States

MONTANA

by Jordan Mills

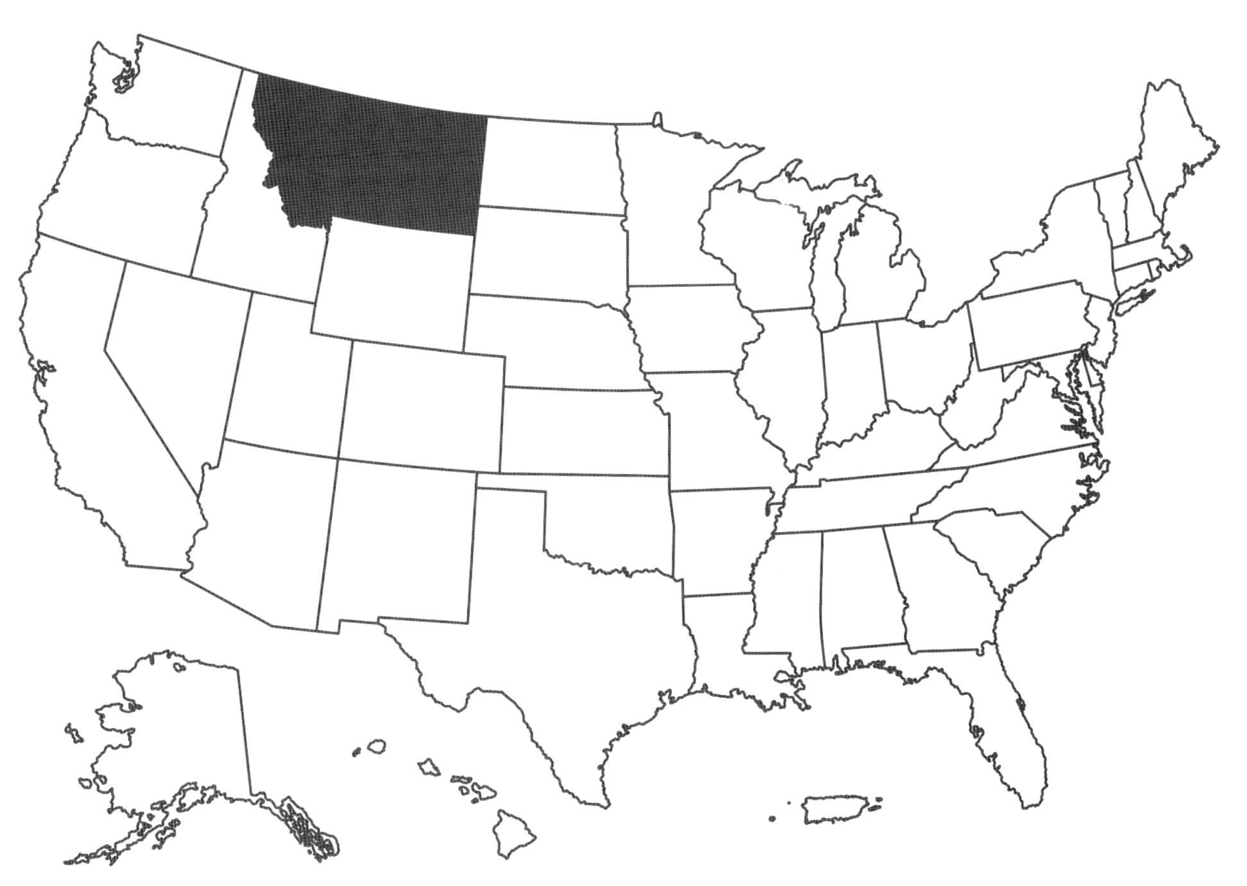

CAPSTONE PRESS
a capstone imprint

Next Page Books are published by Capstone Press,
1710 Roe Crest Drive, North Mankato, Minnesota 56003
www.mycapstone.com

Library of Congress Cataloging-in-Publication Data
Cataloging-in-publication information is on file with the Library of Congress.
ISBN 978-1-5157-0413-3 (library binding)
ISBN 978-1-5157-0472-0 (paperback)
ISBN 978-1-5157-0524-6 (ebook PDF)

Editorial Credits
Jaclyn Jaycox, editor; Kazuko Collins and Katy LaVigne, designers; Morgan Walters, media researcher; Laura Manthe, production specialist

Photo Credits
Capstone Press: Angi Gahler, map 4, 7; Corbis: Historical, bottom 19; Getty Images: American Stock Archive, 12, Michael Ochs Archives, bottom 18, Visuals Unlimited/Ken Lucas, top left 21; iStockphoto: leezsnow, 11; Library of Congress: Prints and Photographs Division, middle 19, 25, 27, 28; Newscom: Album/BULL, CLARENCE SINCLAIR, middle 18; One Mile Up, Inc., flag, seal 23; Shutterstock: 2day, 14, 6015714281, top right 20, Bildagentur Zoonar GmbH, top right 21, Blue Vista Design, middle left 21, Dan Breckwoldt, 17, Dennis Donohue, middle right 21, Galyna Andrushko, bottom left 8, 29, Geoffrey Kuchera, 16, id-art, bottom 24, Images by Maria, top left 20, Jason Maehl, 7, 10, 13, Jiri Vaclavek, middle left 21, Jon Bilous, 5, Kevin Wells Photography, 9, Matt Jeppson, bottom right 20, outdoorsman, cover, 15, Pung, 6, Ronnie Chua, bottom right 8, s_bukley, top 18, Tom Reichner, bottom left 20, xtrekx, top 24; Veronica Wald, top 19; Wikimedia: Internet Archive Book Images, 26, T9500, bottom left 21

All design elements by Shutterstock

Printed and bound in China.
0316/CA21600187
012016 009436F16

TABLE OF CONTENTS

Want to take your research further? Ask your librarian if your school subscribes to PebbleGo Next. If so, when you see this helpful symbol throughout the book, log onto www.pebblegonext.com for bonus downloads and information.

LOCATION

Montana is in the western United States. Montana shares a long northern border with Canada. Wyoming is to the south. North Dakota and South Dakota border Montana to the east. Idaho lies to the west and southwest. Helena is the capital of Montana. The state's biggest cities are Billings, Missoula, Great Falls, Bozeman, Butte-Silver Bow, and Helena.

PebbleGo Next Bonus! To print and label your own map, go to www.pebblegonext.com and search keywords:

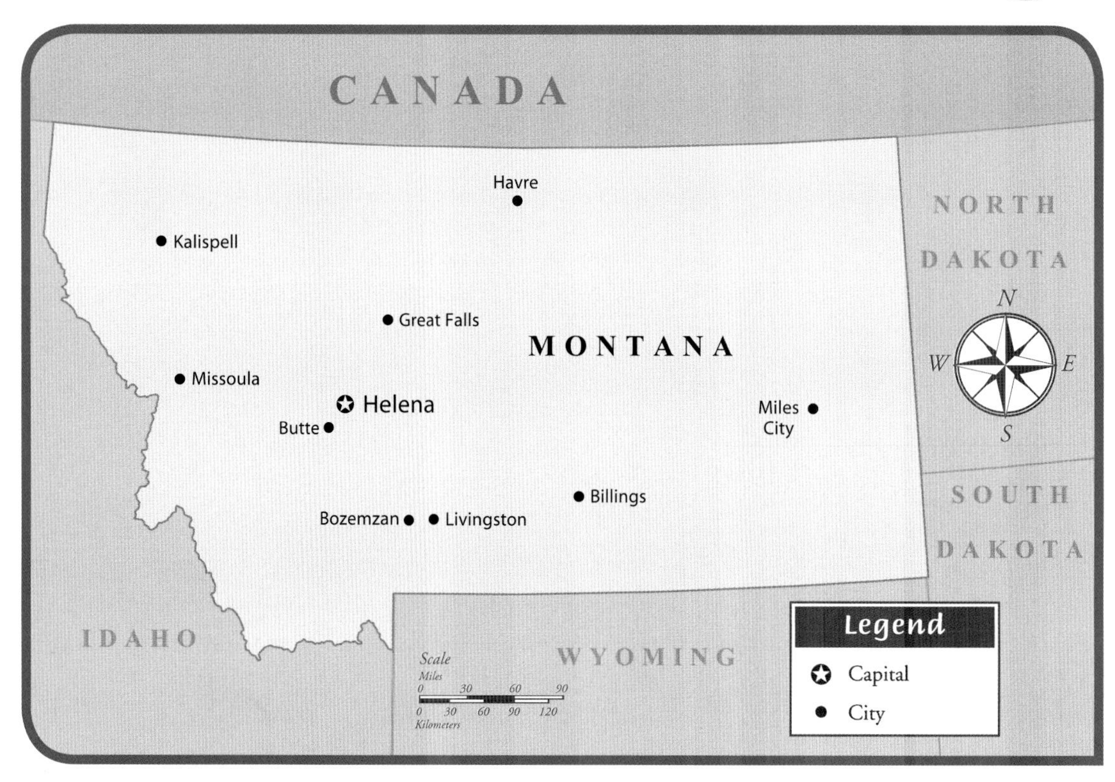

Missoula is nicknamed the "Garden City" for its relatively mild winters.

GEOGRAPHY

Montana has two vastly different landscapes. The Rocky Mountains make up western Montana. The state's highest point is Granite Peak, which is 12,799 feet (3,901 meters) above sea level. Eastern Montana's Great Plains region is grassy and bare. Mostly flat land offers an almost endless view of the horizon. Southeastern Montana has rocky badlands. Wind and water have sculpted rocks here into unusual shapes. Montana's largest rivers are the Missouri and the Yellowstone.

PebbleGo Next Bonus! To watch a video about Montana's landscape, go to www.pebblegonext.com and search keywords:

MT VIDEO

Glacier National Park has over 700 miles (1,130 kilometers) of trails.

Granite Peak is located in the Beartooth Range of the Rocky Mountains.

WEATHER

Montana's climate changes with the region. In winter the plains are cooler than the mountain areas. The average winter temperature is 20 degrees Fahrenheit (minus 7 degrees Celsius). In summer western Montana is usually cooler than eastern Montana. The average summer temperature is 64°F (18°C).

Average High and Low Temperatures (Helena, MT)

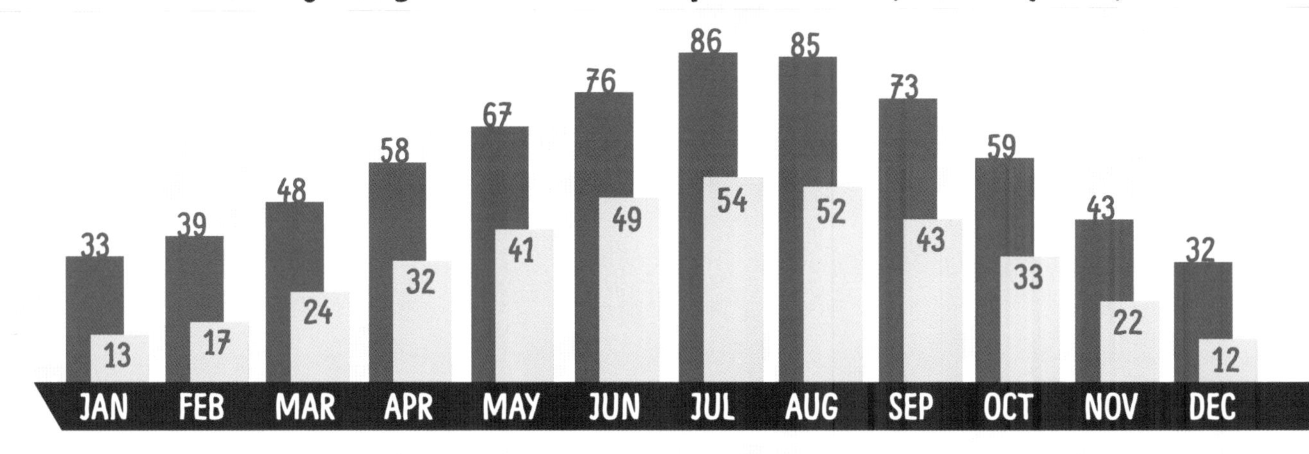

Continental Divide

The Continental Divide snakes through Montana's mountain peaks. East of the divide, all rivers flow eastward. Rivers to the west flow into the Pacific Ocean.

Pompeys Pillar

Pompeys Pillar is a rocky cliff over the Yellowstone River. Hunters met there and scratched their names and drawings in the rock. Explorer William Clark even carved his name there in 1806. It is one of two Lewis and Clark National Monuments in Montana.

Giant Springs

Every day about 390 million gallons (1.5 billion liters) of water flow out of Giant Springs at Great Falls in central Montana. It's one of the largest springs in the world.

HISTORY AND GOVERNMENT

General Custer made his last stand at the Battle of Little Bighorn in Montana.

Before European settlers came to Montana, American Indians lived in the area. Various groups of native people lived on the plains and in the Rocky Mountains. Before the early 1800s, almost no Europeans had been in Montana.

In 1803 the United States bought most of present-day Montana from the French as part of the Louisiana Purchase. Explorers Meriwether Lewis and William Clark arrived in Montana in 1805. In 1864 the U.S. government made Montana a separate territory. On November 8, 1889, Montana became the 41st U.S. state.

Montana's state government has three branches. The governor is the head of the executive branch, which carries out laws. The legislature has two houses, which are the 50-member Senate and the 100-member House of Representatives. These houses make laws. The judicial branch is made up of judges and their courts.

Montana's state capitol building is located between Yellowstone National Park and Glacier National Park, in the city of Helena.

INDUSTRY

Montana's economy still depends on its natural resources, but service industries have become more important. Tourism is now a major industry in Montana. Other service industries include health care, education, retail stores, government, real estate, and finance. Mining and agriculture used to be major industries in the state. Coal, petroleum, and metals are still mined, but the state's mining industry has declined in recent years. Farming and ranching are major industries in eastern Montana. Beef is the state's leading agricultural product.

Many Montana towns were formed because of the timber industry.

Wheat is the state's largest crop. The timber industry is important in western Montana. Most of the state's manufactured products come from raw materials found in Montana. Manufacturing businesses include petroleum refining, lumber and wood production, and machinery and food production.

Cattle ranching in Montana began thriving in the 1860s.

POPULATION

About 90 percent of Montanans have European backgrounds. Many of the state's early settlers moved there from the eastern United States. Others immigrated from England, Germany, Ireland, Poland, and Italy. Today there are about 900,000 white residents in Montana. American Indians are the state's second-largest ethnic group. Many American Indian groups live in the state. These groups are Blackfeet, Assiniboine, Gros Ventre, Crow, Cheyenne, Sioux, Salish, Kootenai, and Chippewa-Cree. Three percent of Montana's population is Hispanic. Asians and African-Americans make up about 1 percent of the state's residents.

Population by Ethnicity

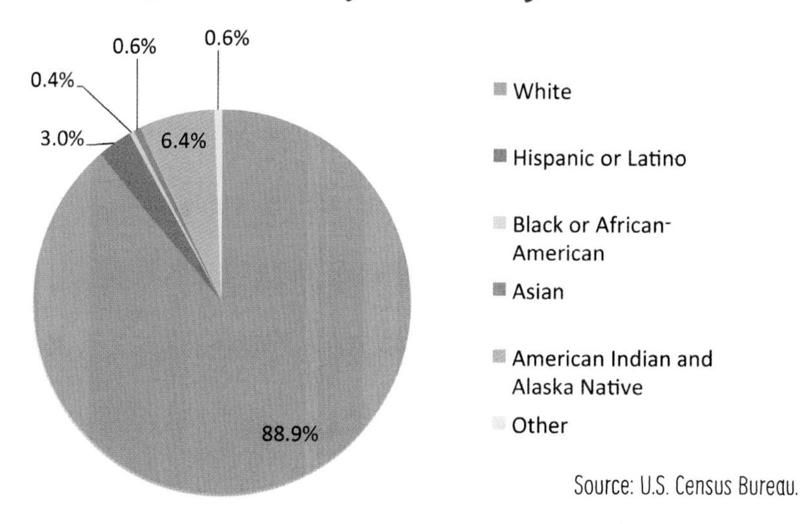

Source: U.S. Census Bureau.

FAMOUS PEOPLE

Dana Carvey (1955–) is a comedian and actor. He began his career on the TV show *Saturday Night Live.* He went on to star in *Wayne's World* (1992) and other zany movies. He was born in Missoula.

Gary Cooper (1901–1961) was an actor known for his adventure movies. Some of his movies are *The Virginian* (1929), *High Noon* (1952), and *Meet John Doe* (1941).

Evel Knievel (1938–2007) was a daredevil motorcycle rider born in Butte. His death-defying stunts included jumping his motorcycle over long lines of cars and deep river canyons. His real first name was Robert.

Norman Maclean (1902–1990) was a writer who wrote about his life in Montana. *A River Runs Through It and Other Stories* is a collection of his stories.

Jeannette Rankin (1880–1973) was the first woman elected to the U.S. Congress. She represented Montana in the U.S. House of Representatives from 1917 to 1919 and 1941 to 1943. She was the only member of the U.S. Congress to vote no to the United States entering both world wars.

Charles Russell (1864–1926) was an artist who painted scenes of American Indians, cowboys, and western landscapes. He was born in Saint Louis, Missouri, and moved to Montana when he was 16 years old.

STATE SYMBOLS

Tree

ponderosa pine

Flower

bitterroot

Bird

western meadowlark

Fish

blackspotted cutthroat trout

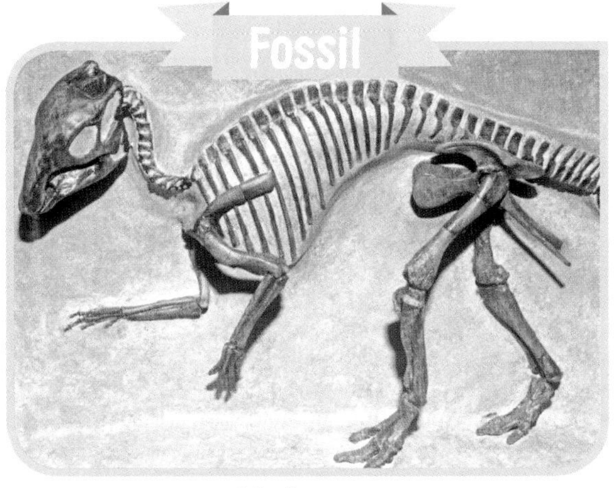

Maiasaura

mourning cloak

agate and sapphire

grizzly bear

bluebunch wheatgrass

PebbleGo Next Bonus! To make a dessert using Montana's main fruit crop, go to www.pebblegonext.com and search keywords:

MT RECIPE

FAST FACTS

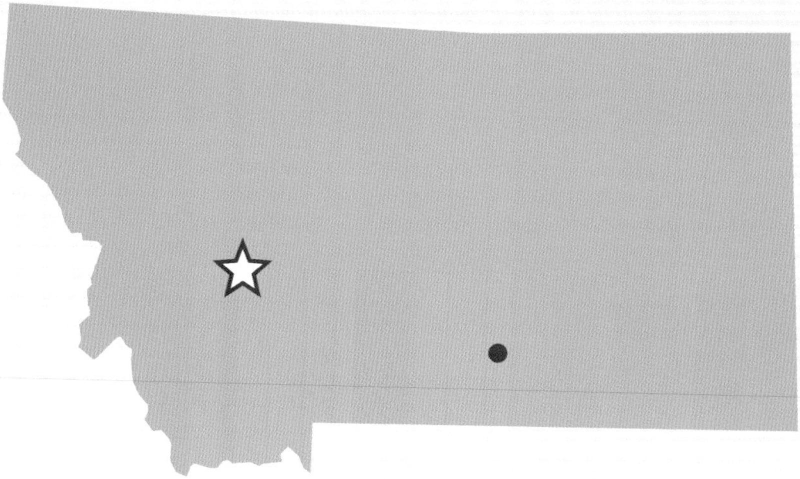

STATEHOOD
1889

CAPITAL ☆
Helena

LARGEST CITY •
Billings

SIZE
145,546 square miles (376,962 square kilometers) land area (2010 U.S. Census Bureau)

POPULATION
1,015,165 (2013 U.S. Census estimate)

STATE NICKNAME
Treasure State, Big Sky Country

STATE MOTTO
"Oro y Plata," which means "Gold and Silver" in Spanish

STATE SEAL

Montana's seal shows the state's history and natural beauty. In the background, the sun rises above the mountains, a waterfall, and the Missouri River. In the foreground, a pick and shovel stand for Montana's mining industry. The plow stands for agriculture. A banner with the state motto, "Oro y Plata," meaning "Gold and Silver," lies below the tools. Around the seal are the words, "The Great Seal of the State of Montana." The seal was adopted in 1965 and has been changed several times.

PebbleGo Next Bonus! To print and color your own flag, go to www.pebblegonext.com and search keywords:

STATE FLAG

Montana's state flag shows the state seal on a blue background. The state's name is printed in gold above the seal. The state seal showcases Montana's history and natural beauty. A banner with the state motto, "Oro y Plata," meaning "Gold and Silver," is at the bottom of the seal. The flag was adopted in 1905.

MINING PRODUCTS

petroleum, coal, copper, natural gas, molybdenum, palladium, platinum, sand and gravel, silver, talc

MANUFACTURED GOODS

petroleum and coal products, food products, wood products, fabricated metal products, chemicals, machinery, nonmetallic mineral products, computer and electronic equipment, printed material

FARM PRODUCTS

livestock, wheat, cherries, sugar beets, hay, barley, potatoes

PebbleGo Next Bonus! To learn the lyrics to the state song, go to www.pebblegonext.com and search keywords:

MONTANA TIMELINE

1620 The Pilgrims establish a colony in the New World in present-day Massachusetts.

1775–1782 Smallpox epidemics kill many Montana Indians.

1803 The United States buys a large area of land from France, including most of present-day Montana. The sale is called the Louisiana Purchase.

1805–1806 Lewis and Clark explore Montana.

1861–1865

The Union and the Confederacy fight the Civil War. Montana is home to many Southern sympathizers, but Northern officials appointed by President Abraham Lincoln govern the territory.

1862

Miners discover gold on Grasshopper Creek in southwestern Montana.

1864

Montana Territory is established.

1872

Yellowstone National Park becomes the nation's first national park. Most of the park is in Wyoming, with small areas spilling over into Idaho and southern Montana.

1876

American Indians fighting relocation to reservations kill General George Armstrong Custer and all but one of his men in the Battle of Little Bighorn in eastern Montana.

1877

The Nez Percé Indians surrender in Montana.

1889

Montana becomes the 41st state on November 8.

1910

Glacier National Park opens in northwestern Montana.

1914–1918

World War I is fought; the United States enters the war in 1917.

1916

Jeannette Rankin from Montana becomes the first woman elected to the U.S. Congress.

1939–1945

World War II is fought; the United States enters the war in 1941.

1972

Montana's new state constitution is adopted.

1989 Montanans celebrate their state's 100th birthday.

2013 Montana's state parks have a record-setting 1.57 million visits between May and September.

2015 Montana hosts its first ever women's-only triathalon.

Glossary

badlands *(BAD-lands)*—areas with many small, steep hills and deep ditches

ethnicity *(ETH-niss-ih-tee)*—a group of people who share the same physical features, beliefs, and backgrounds

executive *(ig-ZE-kyuh-tiv)*—the branch of government that makes sure laws are followed

industry *(IN-duh-stree)*—a business which produces a product or provides a service

legislature *(LEJ-iss-lay-chur)*—a group of elected officials who have the power to make or change laws for a country or state

petroleum *(puh-TROH-lee-uhm)*—an oily liquid found below the earth's surface used to make gasoline, heating oil, and many other products

region *(REE-juhn)*—a large area

sea level *(SEE LEV-uhl)*—the average level of the surface of the ocean, used as a starting point from which to measure the height or depth of any place

smallpox *(SMAWL-poks)*—a disease that spreads easily from person to person, causing chills, fever, and pimples that scar

Read More

Bailer, Darice. *What's Great About Montana?* Our Great States. Minneapolis: Lerner Publications, 2014.

Bjorklund, Ruth. *Montana.* It's My State! New York: Cavendish Square Publishing, 2016.

Ganeri, Anita. *United States of America: A Benjamin Blog and His Inquisitive Dog Guide.* Country Guides. Chicago: Heinemann Raintree, 2015.

Internet Sites

FactHound offers a safe, fun way to find Internet sites related to this book. All of the sites on FactHound have been researched by our staff.

Here's all you do:

Visit *www.facthound.com*

Type in this code: 9781515704133

Check out projects, games and lots more at
www.capstonekids.com

Critical Thinking Using the Common Core

1. Many American Indian groups live in Montana. Name at least two of these groups. (Key Ideas and Details)
2. Tourism is a major industry in Montana. Name three things tourists might want to do or see in Montana. (Integration of Knowledge and Ideas)
3. From 1175 to 1782, smallpox epidemics killed many American Indians in Montana. What is smallpox? (Craft and Structure)

Index